Immigration to America

Identifying Different Points of View About an Issue

Therese Shea

The Rosen Publishing Group, Inc., New York

Published in 2006 by The Rosen Publishing Group, Inc.
29 East 21st Street, New York, NY 10010

First Edition

Library of Congress Cataloging-in-Publication Data

Shea, Therese.
Immigration to America: identifying different points of view about an issue/Therese Shea.
    p. cm.—(Critical thinking in American history)
Includes index.
ISBN 1-4042-0414-8 (lib. bdg.)
1. United States—Emigration and immigration—History.
2. Immigrants—United States—History.
I. Title. II. Series.
JV6450.S47 2006
304.8'73—dc22

2004030295

Manufactured in the United States of America

On the cover: Left: the dedication ceremony for the Statue of Liberty is depicted on the cover of *Le Petite Journal* in 1928. Right: rows of faces of Americans make up this "American flag," which is located at the Ellis Island Immigration Museum.

Contents

Starting Over

Have you ever had a bad day and wanted it to start over? Maybe you thought things could be better if you had another chance. If your one bad day were strung together with many bad days, perhaps you would decide to start over in a new place.

For many people, coming to the United States was a chance to start a new life. People emigrated from other countries for various reasons. Many of the early settlers, even before the colonies in America won their independence in 1783, came to practice their religions without discrimination. In their home countries, they often had to keep their religious beliefs secret for fear of punishment or death. Others had heard about the United States'

Word Works

✓ **emigrate** means to leave one country to settle in another.
✓ **immigrate** means to enter and settle in a country of which one is not a native.

Reread the sentences in which these words are found. What words in the sentences help you to know the difference between "emigrate" and "immigrate"?

These words come from the Latin word *migrare*, which means "to migrate or to move."

available land and growing industries. Many who came from small countries could buy more land at a cheaper price in America than in their home countries. They had a chance to grow wealthy in the United States.

Some people immigrated to America because they had heard about the political freedoms of the United States. They came from countries in which they were not allowed to speak freely and express their opin-

In 1907, immigrants who have just arrived in the United States line up for processing and medical examinations at the immigrant station on Ellis Island in New York Harbor. Nearly one-third of all Americans today can trace their families back to an immigrant who came through Ellis Island, which operated between 1892 and 1924.

ions. Instead, they had to adopt the beliefs of the ruling power. In the United States, people were allowed to keep their opinions. However, not until 1870 and 1920, when amendments to the U.S. Constitution were ratified, did blacks and women have the right to vote and have a voice in their government.

Earliest European Immigrants

When you think of early immigrants in America, you probably imagine Europeans. The oldest American colony was established in 1565 in St. Augustine, Florida, by Spanish explorers.

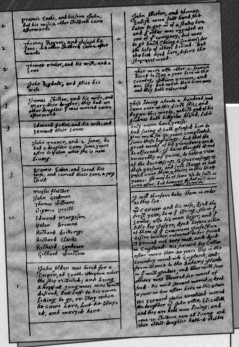

Governor William Bradford included this list of passengers from the *Mayflower*'s 1620 journey to America in his book *Of Plymouth Plantation*.

However, English colonists made up the largest group of early European immigrants. The first successful English colonies were settled in Jamestown, Virginia, and Plymouth, Massachusetts, in the early 1600s.

A small group of English colonists, called Puritans, came to America to practice their

Think Tank

Choose one of the following groups of questions, and answer it in a short essay. Gather a group of four students who chose the same question. Read your essays aloud to each other. Discuss common answers to the questions.

1. Have any members of your family moved to the United States? Interview them. Ask them why they wanted to start a new life in a different country.

2. If you were escaping hard times in a country, what would you hope to find in the country to which you moved? Can you think of possible problems you might encounter in your new country?

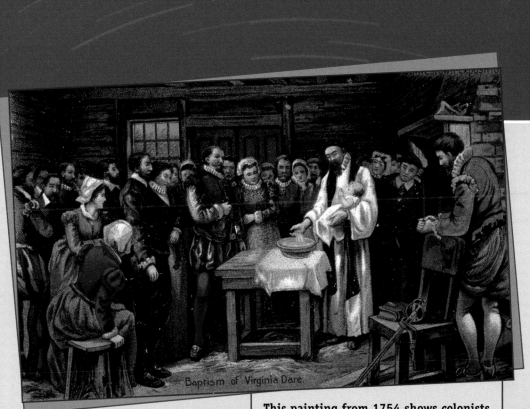

Baptism of Virginia Dare

This painting from 1754 shows colonists on Roanoke Island, Virginia (now North Carolina), and the first child born of English parents in America, Virginia Dare, in 1587. The people of Roanoke disappeared mysteriously, and Roanoke became known as the Lost Colony.

religion freely, away from the Church of England. Later, the Dutch, Swedes, French, Germans, and Scotch-Irish, among others, began arriving. People came to escape disease, wars, and taxes in their native countries. Another problem they encountered in many of their homelands was that land available for farming was rapidly disappearing. Unclaimed land could be found in abundance in North America. Still others came simply seeking adventure and fortune. Throughout U.S. history, most immigrants in America, although they were from different backgrounds, sought the fortune and happiness that they could not find in their native countries.

The Native Americans

When the first European immigrants arrived in America, they did not find a deserted land. There were already people living on the land. The first immigrants were actually the people who are now known as Native Americans. Some scholars say these people came to the Western Hemisphere from Asia by way of an ancient land bridge from what is now Russia to Alaska. Others say they came by sea. Nevertheless, Native Americans were the people who greeted the European explorers and settlers of the New World.

Native Americans showed early European immigrants how to farm the land and shared crops such as potatoes and corn. As more colonists made the journey to America to settle there, and additional lands were needed as settlements and towns grew, many Native Americans were pushed into new territories. With the Indian Removal Act of 1830, the U.S. government forced Native Americans to exchange their

Get Graphic

Based on the Indian Removal Act on page 9, write a short essay that addresses the following:

1. Summarize Section 4 of the Indian Removal Act of 1830 in your own words.

2. Explain how this part of the document later allowed for the removal of Native Americans onto reservations.

3. Explain how the Native Americans and western settlers might have viewed this document differently.

SEC. 4. *And be it further enacted*, That if, upon any of the lands now occupied by the Indians, and to be exchanged for, there should be such improvements as add value to the land claimed by any individual or individuals of such tribes or nations, it shall and may be lawful for the President to cause such value to be ascertained by appraisement or otherwise, and to cause such ascertained value to be paid to the person or persons rightfully claiming such improvements. And upon the payment of such valuation, the improvements so valued and paid for, shall pass to the United States, and possession shall not afterwards be permitted to any of the same tribe.

uncommitted to any other course than the strict line of constitutional duty; and that the securities for their independence may be rendered as strong as the nature of power and the weakness of its possessor will admit, — I cannot too earnestly invite your attention to the propriety of promoting such an amendment of the constitution as will render him ineligible after one term of service.

It gives me pleasure to announce to Congress that the benevolent policy of the Government, steadily pursued for nearly thirty years in relation to the removal

of the Indians beyond the white settlements, is approaching to a happy consummation. Two important tribes have accepted the provision made for their removal at the last session of Congress; and it is believed that their example will induce the remaining tribes, also, to seek the same obvious advantages.

The consequences of a speedy removal will be important to the United States, to individual States, and to the Indians themselves. The pecuniary advantages which it promises to the government, are the least of its recommendations. It puts an end to all possible danger of

(*Top*) Section 4 of the Indian Removal Act of 1830 provided for the purchase of Native American land by the U.S. government. (*Bottom*) This message, written by President Andrew Jackson, was delivered to Congress on December 6, 1830, in support of the act.

much sought-after lands east of the Mississippi River for unsettled lands west of the Mississippi. In the late 1800s, many Native Americans were sent to reservations, areas of land that the government set aside for them. Today, there are about 280 reservations located across the United States.

The Africans

In early America, Europeans first filled the need for workers as indentured servants. These were people who could not afford to emigrate. They promised to work for a certain amount of time. In return, their employers paid for the voyage, provided food and shelter, and released them after the term of work. As early as 1619, traders sold Africans in Virginia as indentured servants. However, as plantations and the crops of rice, tobacco, indigo, cotton, and sugarcane grew, additional laborers were needed.

Why did the use of slaves surpass the use of indentured servants? A person who had an agreement with an indentured servant paid for services that usually lasted four to seven years. Slaves were bought once and became servants for life, as did their children.

The slave trade developed into a cycle called the triangle trade. Slave traders from Europe brought goods such as textiles and guns to Africa and exchanged them for Africans. This part of the slave trade formed one side of the triangle trade. Then the slave traders transported the African captives across the Atlantic to the Caribbean and North American colonies. This is called the middle

Q & A

One difference between indentured servants and slaves was

a. the amount of time they worked.
b. the kind of work they did.
c. the employer for whom they worked.

10

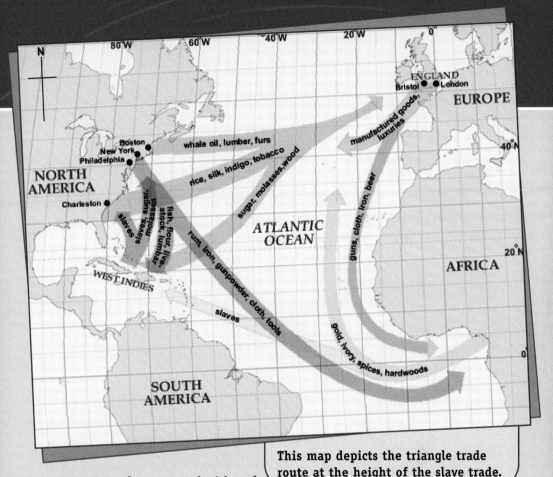

The map labels include:

N

80°W 60°W 40°W 20°W 0°

ENGLAND
Bristol ● ● London

EUROPE

Boston
New York
Philadelphia

whale oil, lumber, furs

40°N

NORTH
AMERICA

rice, silk, indigo, tobacco

Charleston ●

sugar, molasses, wood

ATLANTIC
OCEAN

manufactured goods, luxuries

guns, cloth, iron, beer

20°N

AFRICA

slaves, passage, stock, lumber, molasses

fish, flour, live stock, lumber

rum, iron, gunpowder, cloth, tools

WEST INDIES

slaves

gold, ivory, spices, hardwoods

0°

SOUTH
AMERICA

This map depicts the triangle trade route at the height of the slave trade.

passage, the second side of the triangle. At slave markets, the traders sold Africans or exchanged them for goods. Then the slave traders loaded ships with raw materials that were produced in the colonies and returned to Europe. This trip was the third side of the trade triangle.

The practice of slavery became very profitable for slave owners and slave traders. By 1790, nearly 700,000 Africans lived in the colonies. Of this number, only 9 percent were considered free. It would take many years, the Civil War (1861–1865), and numerous laws before blacks were allowed the same freedoms as others in the United States.

The Irish

At the end of the Revolutionary War (1775–1783), the former thirteen British colonies became known as the United States of America. From 1820 to 1880, more than 9 million immigrants entered this new nation. Among the largest number of immigrants were the Irish, Germans, and Scandinavians who came from the countries of Norway, Sweden, and Denmark.

Almost 3 million of these immigrants were from the small country of Ireland. In 1801, after more than 200 years of war, Britain and Ireland united. Much Irish land was given away to British settlers of Ireland. Even before 1801, the amount of available land to farm had shrunk as the population rose. After the union, only those Irish who swore loyalty to Great Britain could buy and sell land. Furthermore, many Irish Catholics believed they suffered injustices because they were not part of the favored Protestant religion of the English authorities.

Discouraged with the situation, many Irish in the early 1800s boarded ships and

Think Tank

Work in a team with three or four classmates.

1. Examine the picture of Irish immigrants on the next page.
2. Write down several adjectives to describe the situation that is portrayed in the illustration.
3. List several problems that immigrants might have encountered while traveling under these conditions.

Discuss your answers with your classmates.

These emigrants from Ireland had to endure cramped living quarters during their transatlantic voyage to America. Most Irish were restricted to steerage, the part of the ship located below deck that was for passengers traveling at the cheapest rates.

crossed the Atlantic Ocean to America. Before steamships were widely used in the 1880s, the difficult journey by sail could take seven weeks. The large number of people who were packed into tiny quarters below the deck led to the spread of disease. The overcrowded ships came to be known as coffin ships, because many passengers died from starvation and illness.

For those still in Ireland, times became even more difficult. Many poor families depended on the potato crop both for sustenance and for market as a cash crop. Between 1845 and 1850, a disease called the blight spread throughout the potato crop. About 1 million to 1.5 million people died in the famine. Rather than starve, 2 million others left the country during the five-year period. The great numbers of Irish immigrants coming to the United States and Canada did not lessen for many years.

New Kinds of Jobs

Most Irish immigrants could barely afford the long journey across the ocean. When they arrived, their passage was paid for by family members who were already living in the United States or by their future employers. Although many Irish had been rural workers on farms, they had no money to buy farmland when they arrived in North America. They mostly settled near the port at which they landed: New York, New York; Philadelphia, Pennsylvania; Baltimore, Maryland; and the harbor cities of New England, such as Boston, Massachusetts. However, some Irish also traveled inland to cities with plentiful jobs for immigrants, such as Pittsburgh, Pennsylvania, Cleveland, Ohio, and Chicago, Illinois.

New types of work became available in the United States in the 1800s, the age of the Industrial Revolution. Modern methods of transportation such as steamships and railroads required laborers to dig waterways and to lay tracks. In addition, as more factories were built, extra workers were needed to run the machines. The Irish at first took mostly unskilled jobs such as these, which provided them with little money for their often backbreaking work.

Irish immigrants frequently encountered discrimination from

Q & A

According to the text on the next page, some established Americans viewed Irish immigrants in the 1800s as:

a. Untrustworthy

b. Honest

c. Loyal

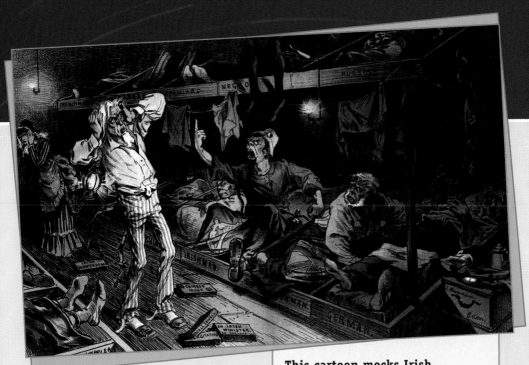

This cartoon mocks Irish immigrants. Many established Americans had prejudice against Irish immigrants because of the immigrants' customs and Catholic religious beliefs.

established Americans who distrusted them because of their Catholic religion and customs. Discrimination became a common occurrence for new immigrants. Americans who had once been immigrants themselves, or who were children of immigrants, were suspicious of newcomers. They especially did not want to lose their jobs to immigrants who would usually work for less money. Signs advertising jobs sometimes read, "No Irish Need Apply." However, as cities grew and the Irish became accustomed to America, they began to find employment as police officers, firefighters, plumbers, and train conductors, among other skilled professions. This change in economic and social status signaled the beginning of much success for the Irish American population.

The Germans

The largest group to arrive in America in the early nineteenth century was from the area now known as Germany. About one-third of all immigrants from 1820 to 1880 were German—more than 3 million people. At this time in Europe, there were many German states that were not yet united. Some Germans left their homelands after an 1848 revolution failed to join the lands. Also many found that they could not pay taxes after crop failures in the 1840s. In the 1870s, many Catholics felt the pressure to leave after German laws were put in place to reduce the power of the Catholic Church in German politics. However, most Germans left their homes because the amount of land available for farming was decreasing.

Many Germans were farmers who passed their land on to one or two of their children or divided the farm into small shares. The population growth in the region meant that the "extra" children either would not inherit land or would inherit a very small piece of land. These young Germans needed to look for different work if they wanted prosperous futures. Although factories were being built and cities were on the rise, many Germans decided to emigrate, choosing the

Paper Works

Read the last paragraph in this section. Then reread the last paragraphs on pages 8 and 9. Think about the effects of new immigrants on the Native American population. Organize your thoughts in a short paragraph.

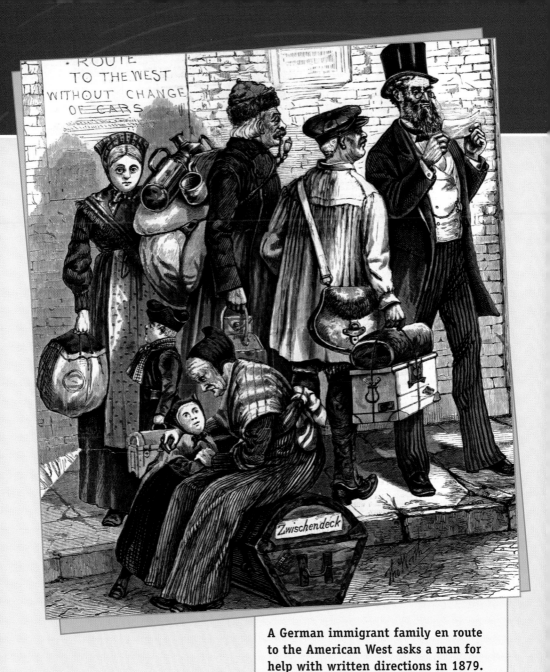

ROUTE
TO THE WEST
WITHOUT CHANGE
OF CARS

Zwischendeck

A German immigrant family en route to the American West asks a man for help with written directions in 1879. Many German immigrants settled in Minnesota, Wisconsin, and Michigan, where they farmed.

United States as the place to re-create their former lives as farmers in the Midwest and West rather than to try to learn new occupations.

The Movement West

Unlike many of the Irish immigrants, German immigrants usually arrived with enough money to travel west, where they purchased land. Early German immigrants settled principally in Pennsylvania. A large number settled in or near the cities of St. Louis, Missouri; Cincinnati, Ohio; and Milwaukee, Wisconsin. These three cities formed a triangle in which the majority of people were German immigrants. In 1857, some Germans went as far west as California, where they founded the city of Anaheim. Many Germans were further encouraged to farm by the Homestead Act of 1862, in which the government offered settlers 160 acres (65 hectares) of western land if the settlers promised to live and make improvements on the land for five years.

German immigrants often tried to keep the ways of their culture by living close to one another and continuing to speak their language. Some German American children in the 1800s attended schools in which all their subjects were taught in German. Because Germany was the enemy of the United States during World War I (1914–1918) and World War II (1939–1945), much

Think Tank

Pair with another student. Have one of you play the role of someone who does not want German taught in American schools during World War I or II. Have the other take the role of someone who wishes to teach or learn German. Each of you will write a short essay, in the form of a letter, to the other. Exchange letters and discuss your arguments.

anti-German prejudice spread throughout the United States. In fact, in Nebraska, a 1920 law called the Reed-Norval Act made teaching not only German but all foreign languages in schools illegal. In 1923, the U.S. Supreme Court declared the law unconstitutional and overturned it.

Those Germans who did not become farmers were skilled in other trades and became bakers, butchers, cabinet-makers, tailors, and beer makers. Germans added

The Homestead Act of 1862 was enacted by the U.S. Congress during the Civil War. The act allowed a person to own land in the west after living and working on it for five years and paying a registration fee.

much to the culture of the United States including music and literature. The fairytales of the Brothers Grimm, German operas, and religious music were shared by German immigrants. German ideas transformed the American education system, including the addition of a kindergarten grade and a gymnasium to school buildings.

The Chinese

Chinese immigration to the United States began in 1848 and increased rapidly when news of the California gold rush reached China in 1849. In fact, people in China heard the news of the discovery of gold before people on the East Coast of the United States did. However, once they arrived in the United States, most Chinese had a very difficult experience in their new homeland during the nineteenth century.

Many of the 300,000 Chinese who immigrated from 1848 to 1882 wanted to make money and return to their native China. A large number of Chinese cities at this time were poor and over-crowded. The stories of *gam saan*, or the "gold mountain," in America were too hard to resist. Many Chinese pledged to work as indentured ser-vants so that they could afford the journey. Some began as laborers in the mines of the American West. Others became fac-tory workers, farmers, or laundry workers. Many, when they had failed to

Q & A

Reread the first sentence in the second paragraph. Answer the questions below.

1. Why did some Chinese wish to come to the United States and plan to return home to China eventually?

2. Why do you think many Chinese could not make money in their new homeland?

3. How do you think American citizens at this time viewed this plan to stay temporarily?

4. How do you view this plan?

This photograph from the 1890s shows Chinese immigrants working on a California railway. More than 60,000 Chinese people, mostly men, came to California during the gold rush of the 1850s. Railroad companies hired many Chinese laborers because they worked quickly and steadily.

find gold in the 1850s, worked laying the railroad tracks of the Central Pacific Railroad, which, when connected to the Union Pacific Railroad at Promontory Summit, Utah, in 1869, became the first transcontinental railroad in America.

Prejudice and Government

As time went on, many Chinese abandoned the idea of returning to their country and settled in American cities. They established neighborhoods called Chinatowns in cities such as San Francisco, California, and New York. The Chinese were often isolated from other people and therefore, easily kept their native language and customs. Some Americans distrusted and disliked Chinese immigrants because they did not understand Chinese customs and their way of dress. They also believed that the Chinese were taking jobs that could go to citizens of the United States.

Acts of government made life even more difficult for the Chinese. First, Chinese miners were taxed through the Foreign Miner's Tax in the 1850s. Then, the Naturalization Act of 1870 made it impossible for anyone not of white or African descent to become a citizen. Another law, the Chinese Exclusion Act of 1882, made it illegal for a period of ten years for the Chinese who did not have immediate family members living in the United States to enter the country. The law was extended for ten more years in 1892 and was made permanent in 1920. Yet Chinese living in America still found ways of

Fact Finder

Write down the title of this page on a piece of paper. Reread the page. List two ways that the United States government exhibited prejudice against Chinese immigrants.

Angel Island in San Francisco Bay in California served as the immigration station for Chinese immigrants from 1910 to 1940. Sometimes called the Guardian of the Western Gate, it was built to control the flow of Chinese immigrants into the United States.

bringing relatives over to the United States, as merchants, teachers, and immediate family members were still allowed to enter. Some Chinese men pretended to be sons of Chinese living in America. The ban was not lifted until 1943 when the U.S. government allowed a small number of Chinese immigrants into the country each year. Today we credit Chinese Americans for introducing various traditions and items to American culture, such as fireworks, barbecue, ketchup, and vaccinations.

Eastern European Jews

Although some Eastern European Jews came to America for the same reasons as other ethnicities—to look for a better life—many were also fleeing for their lives. Most Jews coming to America between 1880 and 1924 were from Russia. Other countries of origin included Austria, Romania, and Hungary.

A dangerous anti-Semitic prejudice was growing in Europe at this time. Many non-Jews were jealous of Jews who had better lifestyles and were suspicious of people who followed a religion different from theirs. This prejudice began to spread via churches and governments. Laws in some countries kept Jews from owning property, having jobs, and even attending school. In 1791, the Russian Empire established the Pale of Settlement. The Pale was a portion of Russia that was set aside for Jews to live in. They could not leave the settlement except under certain legal conditions. Jews were not allowed to enter some Russian

Get Graphic

Write a short essay that addresses the following questions:

a. Which countries surround the Pale of Settlement?

b. Why do you think a special area was created for Jews?

c. How did this area enable pogroms later to easily attack Jews?

AREA OF LEGAL JEWISH
SETTLEMENT IN RUSSIA
IN 1825

Provinces within which Jewish settlement was permitted

Provinces where residence rights were withdrawn in 1825

Kurland Province (and the city of Riga) where new Jewish settlement was forbidden

Zone 50 versts from the western frontiers within which new Jewish settlement was forbidden (about 25 miles)

0   100   200   300
Miles

— Russia Gathers Her Jews: The Origins of the Jewish Question in Russia, 1772-1825 / John Doyle Klier. DeKalb, Ill.: Northern Illinois University Press, 1986.

The Pale of Settlement was a special district within the Russian Empire where Jews were required to live and work from about 1791 to 1917. There were specific laws that the Russian czars used to regulate the Jews in the Pale, hoping to prevent them from living with the general Russian population.

cities such as Moscow. The Russian government even began allowing pogroms (mass killings) against Jews in the early 1900s.

The roads out of their homelands were not easy for many Jews. They had to pass through areas forbidden to them and keep their identities secret. It is estimated that the number of Jews living in the United States before 1880 was around 250,000. By 1924, 3 million Jews lived in America.

Success in a New Land

Many immigrants—such as the Germans, Chinese, and Italians—planned to make their fortunes in America and return to their native countries. The Jews escaping from Eastern Europe and Russia were different because they intended to stay in America. They had no country to accept them back. Jews settled in the urban areas of the Mid-Atlantic (especially in New York), New England, and Midwestern states where jobs were readily available. Many Jews were involved in the clothing industry in cities because these jobs were plentiful. However, working conditions at this time continued to be hazardous. More than 100 Jewish women died in the Triangle Shirtwaist Company fire of 1911 in New York City. The factory building's doors had been locked and there were insufficient fire exits, trapping the employees inside.

Because of tragedies such as this and other sweatshop conditions, many Jews became involved in unions and in social

Word Works

Reread the sentence containing the word "sweatshop." Use the clues in the sentence to answer the following question.

Which is the best definition of the word "sweatshop"?

a. A place where the temperature is very warm.

b. A place where people make shirts.

c. A place where people work long hours for low pay in unhealthy conditions.

work to improve the lives of all immigrants and disadvantaged people. Ernestine Rose, a Jewish American woman, fought for women's rights in the mid-1800s. Louis Marshall, a Jewish lawyer in the late 1800s and early 1900s, is known for being one of the first lawyers to fight for the rights of Jews, Catholics, Asians, and African Americans.

Gradually, Jews improved their lives as a whole and many became successful in their new country. Some became associated with the new motion-picture industry in Hollywood, establishing movie studios such as Warner Brothers. Others became famous musicians and entertainers, including Irving Berlin and the Marx Brothers, whose works are still admired today.

On March 25, 1911, New York City firefighters use their hoses to put out the catastrophic fire at the Triangle Shirtwaist Company in the Asch Building. About 146 workers were killed in the fire, many of whom were young immigrant women. The tragedy led to the passage of tougher factory fire codes.

Italians

People of Italian descent had been among the earliest European explorers. In fact, Amerigo Vespucci gave his name to the continents of North and South America. Yet, before 1880, there were only a few thousand Italian immigrants in the United States.

Between 1880 and 1920, more than 4 million Italians arrived in America. Although more than one-third of these people returned to Europe, a significant number of Italians became American citizens. At this time in Italy, many people were experiencing great poverty because of poor farming methods and absent, demanding landlords. Italians who came to America were mostly too poor to travel farther. They did not often venture past the Mid-Atlantic and New England states. The one exception was in the Midwestern city of Chicago, Illinois, where a large number of Italians settled.

In the cities of these regions, Italians held jobs that had been previously held by Irish immigrants, mainly unskilled factory jobs involving long hours and repetitive labor. Like the Irish, though,

Paper Works

Reread the last full sentence on this page. In a short essay, explain why new immigrants are usually the workforce that is employed in low-paying, unskilled, or dangerous labor.

28

These Italian immigrants are helping to prepare land in New York's Lebanon Valley for railroad tracks, circa 1900.

the Italians became a successful part of the American population. Italians contributed much to American culture, including their love of opera and art. Italian Enrico Caruso became one of the most famous opera singers and was introduced to President Theodore Roosevelt, an enthusiastic fan, in 1906. The paintings of Constantino Brumidi, who was called the Michelangelo of the Capitol, decorated the Capitol building in Washington, D.C.

The Nativist Movement

Italians were often distrusted by more-established Americans, just as other immigrant groups had been. People had exaggerated views of Italian involvement in organized crime. The trial of Italian immigrants Nicola Sacco and Bartolomeo Vanzetti in 1921 for robbery and murder contributed to the spread of negative views of Italians and other immigrants. Even though many people believed that Sacco and Vanzetti had been falsely accused because of their immigrant status, questions about the unrestricted flow of immigrants into the United States were raised.

The ideas once held by the American Party, also called the Know-Nothing Party, a political party that was originally founded in the 1840s, were quickly spreading once again. Members got the name Know-Nothings because when questioned about their ideas, they replied, "I know nothing." The Know-Nothings wanted to restrict the number of immigrants and to make it difficult for these new immigrants to become

Fact Finder

Look carefully at the banner for the American Party. Answer the following questions:

✓ Which president's image is used on this banner?

✓ Why do you think he is shown, as opposed to a later president?

✓ Do you think those who created this banner are really "natives"?

citizens. This was called the nativist movement. Its members considered themselves natives because they were born in the United States.

Soon after the end of World War I in 1918, many Americas worried that the problems that caused the war might extend to the United States. To combat this fear, Congress passed the Immigration Act in 1921, starting a system of quotas for new immigrants. This was called the national origins quota system because an immigrant's chance of gaining entry was based on his or her country of origin. The number of immigrants from each country was restricted to 3 percent of the foreign-born people of that nationality who were already living in the United States in 1910.

The Mexicans

Not all immigrants in the United States traveled across an ocean to get there. From 1820 to 1930, about 750,000 immigrants were from Mexico. Most came after the Mexican Revolution broke out in 1909. Faced with staying in a country that was becoming more violent or entering a nearby country that promised new job opportunities and new lives, many Mexicans crossed the border into the United States.

Mexicans were great assets to the United States during periods of labor shortages. During the two world wars, they filled factory jobs left empty by those who went to Europe to fight. From 1942 to 1964, the U.S. government created programs to

Word Works

"Assimilate" means to adopt the culture of the majority of people in a society.

✓ What other words contain the root "-sim-"? Explain how these words relate to the definition of "assimilate."

✓ At one time in American history, many people thought that the various cultures of the United States should assimilate, or become alike. This was called the melting pot culture. Do you agree with this idea?

encourage Mexicans to enter the country as temporary workers. Farmers could cheaply employ Mexicans as temporary help for their harvests. Nevertheless, this program also allowed farmers to treat the workers unfairly, giving them low wages for long hours of work. Because Mexicans did not have the rights of citizens or legal immigrants, they could do little to help themselves in these unjust situations.

Mexican American Cesar Chavez pickets in 1973. Chavez was a leader of the United Farm Workers of America and a labor activist who worked tirelessly to improve the wages and labor conditions for migrant farm workers.

Mexicans have faced much discrimination by Americans and have been criticized for holding tightly to their culture, including their Catholic religion, ethnic food, and language. Americans who saw this as a rejection of their larger American culture sometimes created rules to encourage Mexicans to assimilate into their culture. For instance, some schools forbade the speaking of Spanish, even at recess. Today, Hispanics, also called Latinos, are the fastest growing population in the United States.

The Puerto Ricans

Puerto Ricans are another major Latino presence in today's United States. Puerto Rico, whose inhabitants have a Native American, Spanish, and African ancestry, has a special connection with the United States. At the end of the Spanish-American War in 1898, the United States annexed Puerto Rico as a colony. Today, Puerto Rico is a commonwealth of the United States. This means that, although it is not a state, it is not an independent country either. Puerto Rico has its own constitution and its own local laws. However, it must observe the federal laws of the United States. Although Puerto Ricans have been considered citizens of the United States since the Jones Act of 1917, they cannot vote in the U.S. presidential election.

Puerto Ricans did not begin arriving in the United States in large numbers until the 1940s. Before airlines made flights to the U.S. mainland affordable for most people, it had been too expensive to travel from the island of Puerto Rico in the West Indies to the mainland United States. In 1910, there were about 2,000 Puerto Ricans living on the mainland United States.

Get Graphic

✓ Use the Internet or an encyclopedia to find the number of Puerto Ricans living in the United States in 1920 and in 1930.

✓ Use this information and the information in this section to create a line graph that shows the changes in Puerto Rican immigration in the United States from 1910 to 1950.

Puerto Ricans welcome spectators to New York City's Puerto Rican Day Parade in June 1985. As U.S. citizens, Puerto Ricans have faced no legal obstacles in migrating to the continental United States. They have had a major impact on contemporary life in America.

In 1940, there were 70,000 Puerto Ricans, and by 1950, more than 225,000 had moved to the United States. More than 3.5 million Puerto Ricans live in the United States according to the U.S. Census of 2000. More than 1 million live in New York City. Puerto Ricans, as did Mexicans, originally flocked to urban areas to fill the jobs left vacant during and after World War II. Similar to that of many Mexicans, their success in the job market is greatly affected by language differences. However, Puerto Ricans continue to improve their lives in America and contribute much to the culture of the United States in politics, athletics, and entertainment. For example, Herman Badillo was the first Puerto Rican to serve in the U.S. Congress, and right fielder Roberto Clemente was the first Puerto Rican to be inducted into the National Baseball Hall of Fame.

The History of Immigration Law

As far back as 1790, U.S. immigration law established that only "whites" could be called citizens. The prejudice against Chinese that was seen in the passage of the Chinese Exclusion Act continued after a 1917 immigration law barred all Asians except Japanese and Filipinos, as well as those with a criminal record, those with certain diseases, and those who were illiterate. In the Immigration Act of 1924, Japanese, too, were blocked as immigrants because the law stated that only people who could become citizens were allowed to enter the United States (and only whites could become citizens). The national origin quota system continued to be enforced, allowing more people from Great Britain, Germany, Sweden, Norway, and Denmark to enter than from any other country. Finally, in 1952, the United States government attempted to correct prejudiced immigration laws. The Immigration and Nationality Act (also called the McCarran-Walter Act) made citizenship available to all people and allowed

Word Works

The Immigration Act of 1917 barred illiterate people from entering the United States. An illiterate person is someone who is unable to read or write.

✓ Think of two reasons why lawmakers included this condition in the act.

✓ Write a paragraph describing your ideas.

The Refugee Act of 1980 enabled people who were fleeing danger in their homelands to enter the United States. These people are called refugees. This photograph shows Cuban refugees in May 1980.

for the immigration of Asians once again, but in limited numbers.

After 1960, Europeans were no longer the majority of immigrants in America. Latin Americans, too, were beginning to move north. In the Immigration and Nationality Acts Amendments of 1965, Congress removed quotas on specific countries and races and instead assigned numbers to hemispheres. It favored relatives of U.S. citizens and those immigrants with special skills. The Immigration Reform and Control Act of 1986 gave illegal immigrants who were living in the country legal status if they applied for it, made employers who hired illegal immigrants pay penalties such as huge fines and serve prison terms, and gave preference to countries that have not sent many immigrants in recent history. The Immigration Act of 1990 raised the number of total immigrants allowed in the United States and rewrote many old laws.

The Future of Immigration

As the origins of immigrants became more widespread, the ways immigrants traveled also changed. People once arrived on boats into immigration checkpoint stations, such as Ellis Island in New York Harbor. Now, they apply for visas in their homelands, file paperwork, and fly by airplane into cities across the United States. Certain ideas have not changed, though. The promise of the United States in the Declaration of Independence to allow "life, liberty, and the pursuit of happiness" continues to lure immigrants to America's shores.

Because the number of immigrants authorized to live in the United States is limited, some people enter illegally. The presence of illegal immigrants causes many debates today. Some people argue that illegal immigrant children should not be allowed to have an education that is paid for by U.S. taxpayers, that illegal immigrants limit job opportunities for citizens, and that government assistance is a drain on tax dollars. Others believe that illegal immigrants deserve some of these things as their basic human rights and argue that the United States is a country founded by immigrants.

The United States continues to be the nation that welcomes

Paper Works

✓ Read a portion of Emma Lazarus's poem "The New Colossus." See http://www.nps.gov/stli/newcolussus/index.html.

✓ Use information from this book about one immigrant group to write an essay stating how this poem describes these immigrants' experiences in the United States.

This 1886 painting of the Statue of Liberty commemorates the unveiling of the statue. The people of France gave the Statue of Liberty as a gift to the people of the United States.

more immigrants than any other country. The Great Seal of the United States contains a Latin phrase—*E Pluribus Unum*—which means "out of many, one." This statement gives Americans hope that the country's many different cultures can exist together as one unified nation.

Timeline

1801	1845	1848	1849	1862	1880	1882	1898	1903

Revolution fails in German states.

Crop failures force millions of Italians to emigrate.

Puerto Rico is annexed to the United States.

Ireland's potato blight strikes, beginning a five-year famine.

The Homestead Act offers land in the United States to settlers.

The Chinese Exclusion Act is passed.

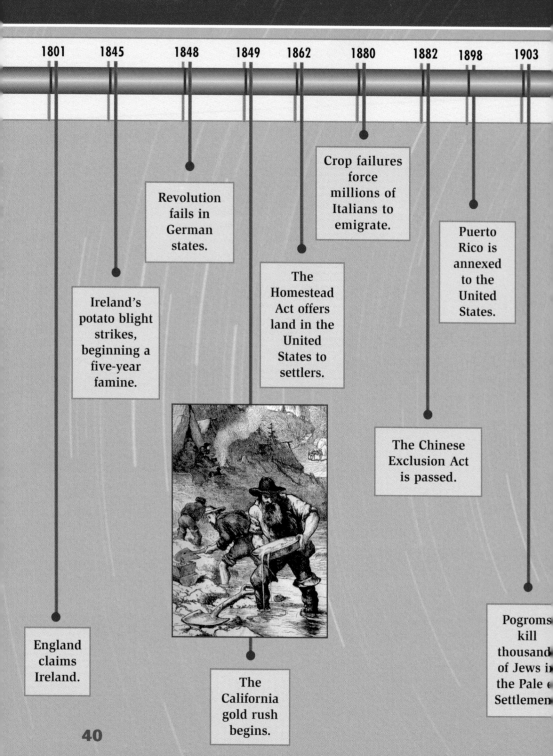

England claims Ireland.

The California gold rush begins.

Pogroms kill thousands of Jews in the Pale of Settlement.

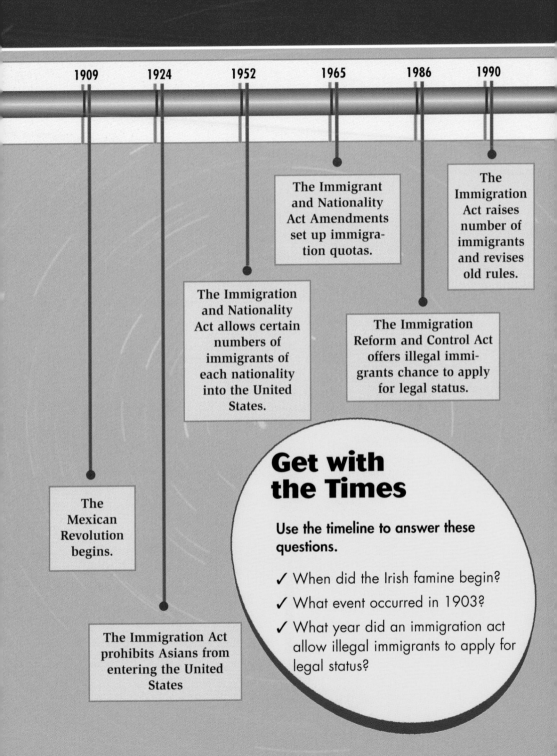

1909

1924

1952

1965

1986

1990

The Immigrant and Nationality Act Amendments set up immigration quotas.

The Immigration Act raises number of immigrants and revises old rules.

The Immigration and Nationality Act allows certain numbers of immigrants of each nationality into the United States.

The Immigration Reform and Control Act offers illegal immigrants chance to apply for legal status.

The Mexican Revolution begins.

Get with the Times

Use the timeline to answer these questions.

✓ When did the Irish famine begin?

✓ What event occurred in 1903?

✓ What year did an immigration act allow illegal immigrants to apply for legal status?

The Immigration Act prohibits Asians from entering the United States

Graphic Organizers in Action

Venn Diagram: Experiences of Irish and Mexican Immigran

Irish (1845)

✓ European origin
✓ Escaped famine
✓ Spoke English
✓ Settled mainly in cities
✓ Immigration slowed in the late 1800s

✓ Took unskilled, low-paying jobs
✓ Faced discrimination due to ethnicity
✓ Spread culture throughout the United States

Mexicans (1909)

✓ North American origin
✓ Escaped war
✓ Spoke Spanish
✓ Migrated to work in factories and on farms
✓ Continue to be largest group of immigrants

Spider Map

IMMIGRATION ACT OF 1924
✓ Permitted no Asian immigration
✓ Allowed more western Europeans than others through national origins quota system

IMMIGRATION AND NATIONALITY ACT OF 1952
✓ Citizenship made available to all ethnicities
✓ Allowed small quota for Asians

FIVE IMMIGRATION LAWS

IMMIGRATION ACT OF 1990
✓ Increased total number of immigrants
✓ Gave protection to immigrants seeking aid from war-torn countries

IMMIGRATION AND NATIONALITY ACT AMENDMENTS OF 1965
✓ Eliminated race and origin as basis of immigration
✓ Established preference system for immigrants

IMMIGRATION REFORM AND CONTROL ACT OF 1986
✓ Offered legal status to illegal immigrants in the United States
✓ Assigned penalties for employers of illegal immigrants

Series of Events Chain: Russian Jews

Anti-Semitic prejudice grows in Russia

Jews in Russia lose many rights affecting their property, education, and employment

Jews are forced to Pale of Settlement in western Russia

Organized pogroms result in many Jewish deaths

Many Jews escape Russia and start new life in the United States

Fact Finder

Choose two other immigrant groups to compare and contrast in a Venn diagram. Look back in the book to complete your chart. Use the summarized information as an outline to write a short comparison essay. In your essay, include ways each group's culture affects your daily life.

Glossary

annex (AN-eks) To add a territory to another territory.

anti-Semitic (ahn-tee SEH-mih-tik) Discrimination against Jews.

assimilate (uh-SIH-mul-layt) To adopt the culture of the majority of people in a society.

commonwealth (KAH-mun-welth) A land that governs itself locally but follows the laws of another government in international affairs and other matters.

emigrate (EH-mih-grayt) To leave one's country to live in another country.

famine (FAHM-in) A severe shortage of food.

illiterate (ih-LIT-uh-ret) Unable to read or write.

immigrate (IH-mih-grayt) To enter and settle a country from another country.

indentured servant (in-DEN-churd SIR-vent) A person who has bound himself or herself to work for another person for a specified time in return for payment of travel and living expenses.

migrant (MY-grent) A person who moves regularly to find work, especially in harvesting crops.

naturalization (na-che-reh-leh-ZAY-shun) The official process by which people acquire citizenship in a country other than the nation of their birth.

pogrom (POH-grem) An organized killing of a group of people.

quota (KWO-tah) A number or percentage that fulfills a requirement.

reservation (rehz-er-VAY-shun) An area of land set aside, especially for Native Americans.

sweatshop (SWET-shop) A place where people work long hours under poor conditions for low pay.

vaccination (vak-sih-NAY-shun) An amount of weak germs given to someone to prevent disease.

visa (VEE-zah) An official permit issued by the relevant authorities that allows legal entrance into a country.

Web Sites

Due to the changing nature of Internet links, the Rosen Publishing Group, Inc., has developed an online list of Web sites related to the subject of this book. This site is updated regularly. Please use this link to access the list:

http://www.rosenlinks.com/ctah/imta

For Further Reading

Freedman, Russell. *Immigrant Kids.* New York, NY: Penguin Group (USA) Inc., 1995.

Hoobler, Dorothy, and Thomas Hoobler. *We Are Americans: Voices of the Immigrant Experience.* New York, NY: Scholastic, Inc., 2003.

Nixon, Joan Lowery. *Land of Hope.* (Ellis Island). New York, NY: Dell Publishing, 1993.

Rodriguez, Consuelo. *Cesar Chavez.* (Hispanics of Achievement). Langhorne, PA: Chelsea House Publishers, 1991.

Sioux, Tracee. *Immigrants in Colonial America.* New York, NY: Rosen Publishing Group, Inc., 2004.

Sioux, Tracee. *Native American Migration.* New York, NY: Rosen Publishing Group, Inc., 2004.

Thornton, Jeremy. *The Gold Rush: Chinese Immigrants Come to America (1848–1882).* New York, NY: Rosen Publishing Group, Inc., 2004.

Thornton, Jeremy. *Immigration and the Slave Trade: Africans Come to America (1607–1830).* New York, NY: Rosen Publishing Group, Inc., 2004.

Yep, Laurence. *Dragon's Gate: Golden Mountain Chronicles: 1867.* New York, NY: HarperCollins Children's Book Group, 1995.

Index

A

Africans, 10–11, 34
American Party (Know-Nothings), 30

B

Badillo, Herman, 35
Berlin, Irving, 27
Brumidi, Constantino, 29

C

Caruso, Enrico, 29
Chinese Exclusion Act, 22, 36
Chinese immigrants, 20–21, 22–23, 26, 36
Civil War, 11
Clemente, Roberto, 35
coffin ships, 13

D

discrimination against immigrants, 14–15, 18–19, 22, 30, 33, 36

E

English immigrants, 6
European immigrants, 6–7, 8, 10, 16, 24, 28, 37

F

Foreign Miner's Tax, 22
freedom, religious/political, 4, 5, 6–7, 16

G

German immigrants, 7, 12, 16–17, 18–19, 26, 36
gold rush, 20, 21

H

Homestead Act of 1862, 18

I

immigration law, history of, 22, 30, 31, 36–37

immigration, reasons for, 4–5, 7, 12–13, 16, 24
indentured servants, 10, 20
Industrial Revolution, 14
Irish immigrants, 7, 12–13, 14–15, 18, 28
Italian immigrants, 26, 28–29, 30

J

Jamestown, Virginia, 6
Jewish immigrants, 24–25, 26–27
jobs available to immigrants, 14, 15, 19, 20–21, 26, 28, 32, 35
Jones Act, 35

L

land availability, 5, 7, 12, 16

M

Marshall, Louis, 27
Marx Brothers, 27
McCarren-Walter Act (Immigration and Nationality Act), 36
Mexican immigrants, 32–33, 35
Mexican Revolution, 32

N

Native Americans, 8–9, 34
nativist movement, 31
Naturalization Act, 22

P

Pale of Settlement, 24
Plymouth, Massachusetts, 6
pogroms, 25
Puerto Rican immigrants, 34–35
Puritans, 6–7

R

Reed-Norval Act, 19
religious discrimination, 4, 12, 24

About the Author

Therese Shea has long been interested in the role of immigration in the formation of the United States, in particular that of her own Irish and German ancestors. She earned a M.A. in English education from the State University of New York-Buffalo. She has taught high school English and currently writes and edits science, history, and math books and curricular materials in Buffalo, New York.

Photo Credits: Cover (left and right), pp. 5, 13, 17 © Corbis; p. 6 courtesy of the State Library of Massachusetts; p. 7, 40 © Getty Images; p. 9 (top) courtesy of the Library of Congress; pp. 9 (bottom), 19 © National Archives and Records Administration, Washington, DC; pp. 11, 25 © Perry-Castañeda Library Map Collection/Historical Maps of the Americas/The University of Texas at Austin; pp. 15, 23, 33, 37 © Bettmann/Corbis; pp. 21, 27 © Underwood & Underwood/Corbis; pp. 28–29 © Michael Maslan Historic Photographs/Corbis; p. 31 © David J. & Janice L. Frent Collection/ Corbis; p. 35 © Owen Franklen/Corbis; p. 39 © Museum of the City of New York/Corbis.

Designer: Nelson Sá; Editor: Kathy Kuhtz Campbell
Photo Researcher: Nelson Sá